RECLAIMING THE SOUL

By
Dr. W. Tom Wiseman &
Dr. Theresa J. Bowen

PublishAmerica
Baltimore

First printing

ISBN: 1-4137-1631-8
PUBLISHED BY PUBLISHAMERICA, LLLP
www.publishamerica.com
Baltimore

Printed in the United States of America

This book is dedicated to all Vietnam veterans,
their families and friends.

CONTENTS

CHAPTER 1

GOING BACK

Too many feel guilt and shame,
and too few pride and honor.
Too many fought too bravely;
too few had the sense to run,
Too few made it home alive,
and too many never did.
Patrick P. Stafford, *VIETNAM THESIS*

I have always thought about going back to Vietnam. "Why in the hell do you want to go back?" came from one bar stool, in VFW post #3360, Defiance, Ohio. Why would anyone want to go back? After all it had been nearly thirty-three years, and many of the memories were not good! But it had been something that had been in our minds off and on for years. So when my ole high school buddy and Marine Corps colleague, Bill Steffan called and said that his daughter, Janna, was on a world cruise (Semester at Sea), and one stop was in Vietnam; Bill and I made our plans.

About a month prior to the trip, I ran into Tom Reed (Rebo) an old friend and decorated Vietnam Marine Veteran at the VFW Post #3360. Tom proudly announced, after we had slammed a few beers that he, too, was going to join us on the trip. Frankly, I thought it was the beer talking because he did not have a passport, Visa, or for that matter, had not even checked into availability of airline tickets. But, very much to our surprise, he booked a flight, obtained the required documents and within just a few days of departure paid premium price to travel via Thailand, due to the lateness of securing flight reservations.

Returning to Vietnam is a fairly straight forward and a simple process. As mentioned earlier, Bill called and invited me to go with him. Now, I should explain that Bill has an MBA and has done quite well for his family and himself. Bill is frequently involved in multi-million dollar deals, bailing out struggling companies and fixing things professionally in the business world. I, on the other hand, still owe $26,000.00 on my graduate school loans and as a college professor I am still trying to figure out how to pay my utility bills every month. I told Bill, no matter how in debt it would take me, he could count on me!

The required documents for travel are relatively easy to obtain. The first step in the process is to obtain a passport. In many states a passport application can usually be obtained at the county courthouse. The United States Federal Government issues the actual passport. You will need two passport approved pictures which are usually less than $20.00 at most Wal-Mart, K-Mart or Meijer stores. The cost of the passport is usually less than $80.00 and one can allow a minimum of 45 to 60 days for processing. The passport will be your key to traveling to and from the United States. A second document that you will need will be a VISA, which is issued by the government of Vietnam. Visa applications need to be submitted to the Vietnam Embassy in Washington D.C. You will need to submit one passport picture and your passport with your VISA application. The cost is approximately $65.00. One should allow a minimum of four weeks for processing. A Visa application can be downloaded from most Vietnam websites or simply search in Vietnam Travel. Just a little helpful traveler's tip, while traveling, and particularly while in the country, carry your passport/Visa in a secure pocket. Perhaps the best way is to sew a pouch inside of your shorts or slacks.

Keep in mind that Vietnam is halfway around the world from the United States and an estimated flight time from the lower 48 is about 18 hours. Remember, you are much older than when you first traveled there. It is a long trip and it does affect the internal clock, but the good news is that the time difference is exactly 12 hours. This makes it easy to know the time in the U.S. and in Vietnam without having to reprogram your watch. For example, when it is 8:00 P.M. Monday in Vietnam it is 8:00 A.M. on Monday in New York. Once all the paperwork is in order, you are ready to go. Since Bill, Rebo and I had everything in place, we were ready for this big trip. Well, sort of…

Few would argue that the Vietnam War was divisive. Not since the Civil War had this country known such division. Many in these United States in the 1960's and 1970's felt compelled to choose between conscience and patriotism. Ultimately, lines were drawn in the sand from college and university campuses to the streets of our cities and even in rural America. There were anti-war protesters on one side and those supporting the cause on the other side. Now, thirty years since the war has ended, the burning questions of the day seem to be some of the same as those of ages past. Which side was right? What has happened to the war veterans from both sides? What do they think today? This book will attempt to answer these and other questions that both American and Vietnamese veterans seem to be asking themselves more frequently, as the years pass by.

To answer these questions, it was decided that it would be best to interview former N.V.A (North Vietnamese Army) and V.C. (Viet Cong) war veterans, and by talking to the very people who were most impacted by the war. Namely, the parents and family members from both sides who lost loved ones as a result of the conflict. For the United States, the war involvement ended in 1973 with the culmination of the Paris Peace Talks.

A lot can happen in thirty years! After all, in the thirty-year period between 1876 and 1906 this nation experienced Custer's last stand and the first successful flight in an airplane by human beings. Likewise, in a thirty-year period, people can also significantly change. We have all probably heard the old saying that people, like wine usually mellow with age. Our trip to Vietnam would provide an excellent barometer to test this theory and help us to learn the philosophy, temperament and beliefs of the Vietnamese people today. Nonetheless, a return trip back to Vietnam was not without much contemplation and apprehension. Although, prior to the trip we were too vain to admit it, we later all agreed that there was a good deal of fear on each of our parts, traveling and returning to such a place of unpleasant memories.

If there were to be a disclaimer regarding going back to Vietnam, it would clearly have to be: "It is not for everyone!" After all, WWII veterans have had more than 55 years to heal, and many of them after that period of time continue to choose not to return to their "place of war." Considering that equation into the mix, it makes sense that those who have had less time to heal (in the case of Vietnam veterans) may not be ready to return. But for those who do choose to go back, there are a few things that we would like to share with you. These tips might be worth knowing to help you better prepare for your return, and make the process a bit less of a concern for you.

Perhaps one of the biggest surprises we found on our return trip was the attitude of the Vietnamese people toward Americans. Surprisingly, most of the Vietnamese people living in Vietnam, today, were not alive during what they refer to as the "American War." Statistically, it is estimated that of the 80,000,000 Vietnamese people who occupy the 128,275 square miles of Vietnam, about two-thirds or approximately 56,000,000 were born after the war. This of course means that the majority of the people have no memory of the conflict. Additionally, we found that those who were alive during the war, today, make the conscience choice not to remember.

Of course, there are exceptions as we discovered the first night in Ho Chi Minh City. You remember it as Saigon. (Many communities throughout Vietnam were renamed after the war by the government). Staying at a very nice and rather affordable hotel, The Saigon Hotel also known as The Best Western Chancery Saigon All Suite Hotel, we did encounter a bit of opposition. While sitting at the hotel bar drinking a "Tiger Beer" the Mama-san behind the bar asked me where I was from. After telling her the United States, she asked me if I was there on business. My response was a simple. "No, I was here in Vietnam during the war with the United States Marines." She promptly gave me the thumbs down sign and said, "BAD! BAD!"

In the corner of the room came a husky voice with a heavy German accent belonging to a man shaking his fist in the air and proclaiming, "Yeah, we were over there in Germany saying Ho Chi Minh, Ho Chi Minh!" Without thought, I turned to the man, looked him straight in the eyes and said, "That's okay, but I'll bet when my dad's generation was taking out Hitler, you guys were not chanting Adolph Hitler, Adolph Hitler!! The gentleman paused, smiled, listened and then bought me a beer. Privately that evening, at least three Vietnamese who observed the incident thanked me for what the Americans did.

Basically, the country and people of Vietnam are not what you left thirty years ago. The infrastructure is such that people for the most part no longer live in thatched huts or tin and pallet constructed dwellings; not even those who reside in what used to be primitive rural villages. Rather, today most people live in houses, which appear to be constructed of a masonry type material very similar to the houses that would be found in say, parts of

Florida or Southern California. Even more surprisingly, nearly every place that we visited people had running water, electricity and sewers.

Many of the cities, likewise, have changed significantly. For example, Phu Bai has a four-lane state of the art highway supporting a magnificent lighted boulevard that would rival any found in the United States. Hue is an attractive and well-manicured city that supports a large visitor's bureau and welcome center. Quang Tri currently is under a major renovation project (sewers, sidewalks, etc.) and supports a U.S. flag and Vietnam flag flying jointly at the headquarters of an international business located there.

Saigon or Ho Chi Minh City was, in fact, the busiest center of all the places we visited. Currently, the population is about four million and the traffic is horrendous. Small motorcycles, bicycles and a few automobiles, but the majority are not American made. Yes, you do still see families of four traveling on 50 and 90 cc motorcycles. The two prevalent things about the traffic in Saigon are that people travel whatever direction they choose. For example, unlike the United States where drivers must remain on the right side of the road, people in Vietnam travel on whichever side they choose. The other thing is that there are very few traffic signals. Therefore, if one chooses to cross the street, it is done without looking right or left. In fact, drivers are expected to avoid pedestrians. Truthfully, it is difficult to understand why there are not more vehicle and pedestrian accidents. While it is true that traffic is the worst thing about Saigon, without a doubt the best thing is the friendly people.

DaNang is also a city of bustling activity, traffic and people. However, it is not as populated, nor is the infrastructure as advanced as in Ho Chi Minh City. Actually DaNang is a relatively dirty city due to dust from traffic traveling unpaved roads or paved roads with gravel and dirt shoulders. DaNang took some pretty heavy damage from military action after the U.S. troops pulled out in the 1970's. Today, there is little evidence of U.S. military involvement in DaNang and, for that matter, throughout Vietnam. Although there is an occasional military vehicle such as a jeep or deuce and a half truck passing by, the only other exception would be at the war museums that are found in Ho Chi Minh City, DaNang and Hanoi.

These war museums are probably the major source of anti-American propaganda found today in Vietnam. It was difficult at best to view the rusted remains of U.S. Military helicopters, planes, tanks, and artillery. It was also difficult to think of the Americans who actively maintained and operated these military pieces of equipment. Yet, perhaps the most difficult part of the visit to the war museum was the pictures of American Soldiers holding the severed heads of "Viet Cong" in their hands. The deformed bodies of *Agent Orange* victims, the piles of dead bodies, (many of whom were children killed at the My Lai Massacre) these museums are grim reminders that war is ugly! Yet, one must remember that these types of things occurred on both sides.

Of all of the major cities, Hanoi is by far the most modern. This is probably in part due to the rebuilding of the city after the many years of intense bombing. According to some records, more bombs were dropped on Vietnam in 1970 than were dropped in all of World War II. As a result, the infrastructure is relatively new and in fine shape. This might also be due, in part, to the fact that the climate is so mild. Unlike, say Minnesota or Northern Ohio, where winter weather combined with the use of salt and other ice and snow melting chemicals eat away at infrastructure; the Vietnamese city infrastructure is protected.

Essentially, Hanoi supports one of the nicest modern airports we have ever seen. The highly polished floors, state of the art ticketing process and overall cleanliness would rival any U.S. airport. The Saigon, formally Ton Son Nuit and the DaNang airports were not nearly as nice. The DaNang airport is not much more than an old building without any amenities. Nonetheless, airline service in Vietnam is conducted very similar to that in the United States. Security is heavy; and baggage and passport checks are highly scrutinized. We found out just exactly how quickly security could respond at the Hanoi Airport when Rebo pulled a "Tiger Beer" from his carry on baggage and began to consume it.

Yes, our trip to Vietnam provided an excellent opportunity to experience the country as it is today. But for us, the greatest experience of all was talking to the people who lived and participated in the war: former Viet Cong, former North Vietnamese Army Regulars, former South Vietnamese soldiers, mothers who lost sons and daughters in the conflict and even former American combat military participants who we met while in this country. Their stories follow.

CHAPTER 2

DONG'S STORY
GRANDFATHER NOW

This is the story of Dong, a former Viet Cong (V.C.) who lives in DaNang. Dong was the first of former enemy soldiers that we encountered. At age 59, Dong has lived a rather long life given the fact that the average life expectancy in Vietnam today is 63 years. Given his age, Dong is a rather spry man having the appearance of a 40-something-year-old. Like many Vietnamese, he is rather short, standing about 5'6" in his stocking feet and quite slim weighing about 130 pounds. The only hint of his true age would be the deeply embedded laugh lines embedded around the corners of his eyes and the mixture of white and black tarnished teeth.

Dong's overall appearance was one of confidence; his dress was very similar to that of Vietnamese people some 30 years ago. He wore black, silk pants; a white, silk shirt, and a baseball cap along with a straw-coned shaped, woven hat to protect him from the sun. Dong spoke excellent English and when he did talk, it was always in a very loud voice, usually using hand gestures to make his points. He seemed to be a rather content man, very friendly and extremely enthusiastic.

Dong told us that he has lived in the DaNang area most of his life, with the exception of the time he lived in north Hanoi. His time in Hanoi was spent in military training to become a trainer of other V.C. forces. After his training, he told us he was sent back to DaNang where he spent much of the war training local Viet Cong sympathizers. When we found Dong, he was operating a parking area for motorcycles at China Beach, next to the beautiful five-star resort. The day we met up with Dong, we had driven to China Beach to check out the view. We were not disappointed as we did enjoy a magnificent view.

China Beach is located just a few minutes from the heart of DaNang City. The shining, white sand of the beach and the beauty of the scenic Monkey Mountain highly compliment the sparkling, deep blue water of the South China Sea. Our guide informed us that at one time Monkey Mountain was occupied and home to many monkeys, but many were killed during the war and probably eaten by the V.C. Nonetheless there are still monkeys inhabiting "Monkey Island." Perhaps one of the neatest things about China Beach is that it is as about as close to being westernized as you will get in Vietnam. People in bathing attire, sitting at bamboo umbrella covered tables, along the waters edge, in between the nicely manicured palm trees, sipping tropical drinks and drinking any of the major American brews that one might find in American venues.

Having the unique opportunity to sit down and talk with Dong might well be one of the two major highlights of our trip. He spoke to us very candidly and when speaking about the war, he almost never broke from his smile. Yet, he spoke with sincerity and even with a sense of respect. Sitting face to face with a former V.C. and being in a position to ask questions was indeed a time for one to be cautious not to "mess up" the rare opportunity. So we explained to Dong about our research for the book and he agreed to answer any questions the best he could.

To the question, "Did you fight in the war? He answered with an overwhelming, "Yes!" He said he fought for many years, but was not actually sure how many he did serve, in part due to the fact that he was a Viet Cong and therefore participated in the war on an intermittent basis. Likewise, to the question, "Did you belong to a particular military organization? His answer was similar. He explained that unlike the North Vietnamese Army Regulars who were assigned to a specific unit or outfit, he as a Viet Cong did not belong to an organized group. When asked the question, "Did you hold a specific rank? He smiled and said, "I had no rank, like those in the North Vietnamese Army. I was just a person who believed in the cause and wanted to do my part."

The next question asked of Dong was, "How many years did you actually serve?" Once again, he said he was not completely sure, but remembered working for the cause when he was 12 years old. That would calculate to have been sometime around 1954 when the French were still engaged in conflict with the Vietnamese people. He went on to say that he actively participated in some ground combat operations between 1965 and 1975; however, the majority of those years were spent in organizing and training others to become Viet Cong gorilla fighters.

When asked, "What areas did you participate in terms of combat operations?" He replied, "Mostly in the area that the United States troops called I Corps. (I Corps was primarily composed of the northern section of South Vietnam). He explained that a good deal of his activity occurred in the DaNang area. This area was highly occupied by U.S. Marine and U.S. Army personnel. Dong said most of his work was done at night with the exception of the activities that required or were best served in daylight hours. He explained that there was little money, few weapons and very few supplies to arm those being trained as Viet Cong. Much of the equipment supplies that were used to meet local training needs came from area sympathizers. Nonetheless, Dong said, "Somehow they were always able to get what they needed when the need was there."

Then we asked the big question to Dong: "Were you angry with the American combat troops during the war?" His response was almost without thought and for the first time he broke his smile. "Yes, I was very angry!" He then talked about the many friends and family that he lost during the war years. "It was for us, you see, a hard time. We were involved in a war very similar to your country's civil war. The U.S. troops coming here to my country and getting involved would have been no different if the people of France or Mexico would have gotten involved in your war, fighting for the south." Dong went on to explain, "Ours was an internal conflict just like yours! An internal conflict that should have been allowed to be solved by us, after all, it was our country!"

Now that many years have passed since America withdrew from Vietnam, are you still angry? Have you been able to forgive the Americans combat troops? Dong quickly responded, "We do need to be friends now." When asked about what sort of relationship should our countries have and whether or not they should work together, he replied, "Yes, our countries should work together, it would be best for all!"

Did Dong believe that America or Vietnam won the war? He replied, "Vietnam won the war because the people of Vietnam love their country." He went on to explain even though America had superior weapons and aircraft, he believed that America lost the war because the people of the United States did not want the war.

How did Dong feel about former American personnel returning to Vietnam today? Did he think it was good or bad? He told us, "It is a good thing that American veterans come back so that we can be friends. In the war you did what you were told and we did what we were told and now WE FIGHT NO MORE! We now can be friends and work together."

We told Dong about the many veterans organizations that we have in the United States such as the DAV, Veterans of Foreign Wars, American Legion and the AMVETS and how they assist veterans and their families in obtaining benefits. Did Vietnam have such organizations to help their veterans? He told us that he was not aware of any and that most of the time veterans in his country would just get together from time to time and talk.

The day was getting late and it was time for us to head for the airport as we were taking the hour plus flight to Hanoi that evening. So we thanked Dong for his time, Rebo gave him some money for letting us park our rented motorcycles in his parking lot and we started to leave. As we were leaving I asked Dong a question that was not a part of our survey. You are 59 years old and people in this country only live to be on the average of 63, what do you like to do now that you no longer must fight? He smiled and answered with an answer I shall never forget. "I like to spend time with my grandchildren."

Suddenly, my thoughts reverted halfway around the world to my own grandchildren, but not before a tear moistened the corner of my eye. For the first time it truly hit me, and suddenly I realized that we former enemies really wanted the same thing. We both wanted to be GRANDFATHERS NOW.

CHAPTER 3

DENNIS O.
THE WALKING DEAD!

Time, Dateline TET Offensive, 1968, Vietnam. It sounds like an Audie Murphy film, he was twice wounded from enemy fire, his unit overran at Khe Shan, twenty-six ribbons, medals and decorations including the Purple Heart. He took a 45-caliber pistol and alone crawled out to the wire when some of his men thought they heard noises like snipers coming through. As a platoon staff sergeant, when the outpost was being overran, he led two guys from each squad to get ammo because the ammo supply was exhausted.

Dennis Owen Schaffner, a member of the legendary 1st Battalion 9th Marines known by many as the "Walking Dead," a name said to be earned because three times the outfit came under fifty percent strength due to causalities, KIAs and tour rotations. Dennis Owen Schaffner a man who tried to quit a couple of times, but his will and the people who cared about him, namely his loving wife Pat, would not let that happen.

(Dateline, Defiance, Ohio) Denny, a past acquaintance from 1971, when he was a New York Life Insurance Agent was aspiring to assist newly discharged veterans in converting their GI insurance. He was a pleasant person to be around, full of smiles and gentle, kind words. But inside, there was a blemished, scarred man masking the pain of wartime experiences. Dennis O, although no longer with the "Walking Dead" was now among the "Walking Wounded." Yet, Denny at VFW or DAV meetings, always appeared very sincere in his interest to assist veterans in need.

As he continued to be involved with assisting veterans in obtaining Veteran's Administration Benefits, Dennis became an incredibly heavy smoker, heavy drinker, and did not stay at one job for any length of time. His work performance was beyond question and his employers were always quite satisfied with his management style, but after a while Dennis would become restless and want to move on.

Dennis was also struggling in his marriage. Now most would agree that Pat, his loving wife, was always, by all accounts, for being of good judgment, but even her limits were severely tested a couple of times because of Denny's behavior. A couple of Driving Under the Influence charges, quitting jobs, staying out and driving home when his level of intoxication was not only beyond the legal limit, but also beyond sanity and medical safety was many risks he would take. Gambling, playing tickets of chance, often spending more money then he could afford was a constant problem. Yet, no one can take away the fact that Dennis was always a fine father and dependable friend. In spite of all of his efforts he just simply could not erase the residuals of the war, believed to be Post Traumatic Delayed Stress Syndrome. That is until a few years ago when a new Dennis O. or perhaps the pre-Vietnam Dennis O. surfaced.

It was in the early 1980's when his wife, Pat as Denny now states, "Literally made me go to church." It was then when many first noticed the change in Denny. His increased involvement in assisting and attending to those less fortunate was testimony in itself. We already mentioned his commitment to needy veterans and their families, but actually that dedication grew into what is now more than 25 years of leadership and involvement in organizations to benefit those "Walking Wounded" out there. For example, Dennis took on a leadership role with the local Salvation Army, serving on the board of directors. Not only did he stand in front of the local mall and ring the bells at Christmas time, but he also helped to make the organization one of the bigger recipients of charitable donations in the area. He raised money that was used for such critical needs as helping the homeless and feeding the hungry. After building the coffers of the local Salvation Army organization, this newfound Dennis O. took on a major leadership role in raising funds to build the first and only Y.M.C.A in the Defiance, Ohio community.

Yes, Dennis evolved into the type of citizen that every local elected official wants and seeks for their community. Today he remains increasingly active promoting the cause of veterans, their widows' dependent children and orphans by his involvement in the Defiance, Ohio area Veterans of Foreign Wars, American Veterans Organization, Disabled American Veterans, American Legion, Marine Corps League and Purple Heart Association.

Through hard work and determination, Dennis overcame his self-proclaimed demon of alcohol and the residuals of the war. This new Dennis O. has served as keynote speaker for regional and state conferences. He is recognized statewide for his commitment to the less fortunate and particularly to veterans. He established a homeless shelter and on many occasions slept there as a volunteer. Perhaps the most impressive thing that we have seen Denny do was to take the last dollar out of his pocket and give it to a cold, hungry person down on his luck.

If you ask Dennis, he would likely tell you that the religious song that best describes his journey would be *Amazing Grace*, particularly the words, "I once was lost and now am found, was blind and now I see." If you would ask those of us who know him we would say Dennis O. Shaffner is a true patriot, Christian and hero; the type of man his community can be proud of….

CHAPTER 4

QUANG
A SOUTH VIETNAMESE VETERAN

What did happen to the South Vietnamese veterans? Where did they go and what are they doing today? What about the civilians who worked on American military compounds? Answers to these questions eluded us for a good deal of our trip until we met up with an elderly gentleman named Quang. Quang had an excellent memory of the American involvement, particularly in I Corps. He had served in the South Vietnamese Army, but was discharged after being severely wounded from Viet Cong rockets. After his discharge, he worked on several American military compounds, driving trucks, hauling garbage and doing whatever was asked of him. He could recite from memory the location of nearly every major military unit in the providences of Quang Tri and Quang Nam (DaNang area).

Today, Quang and his family still reside in the Quang Nam providence. He proudly declares that he has been married for thirty-five years to the same woman. Additionally, they have six children; all of whom arc now adults. He and his family appear to live at a fair standard of living given his former loyalty to America. By our best guess, his success can be attributed to his willingness to work long and hard over his lifetime. Another reason may be that his children, although grown, continue to reside together and pool their resources, including income.

So what has happened to those who served in the South Vietnamese cause? The answer is really twofold. During the last days of the war, those who were able, escaped by means of

American assistance. Unfortunately, as revealed in the news footage of the 1975 evacuation of the U.S. Embassy, many were left behind to meet such a fate as imprisonment, torture or worse–execution. Many South supporters tried to reach the safety of neutral ground by using overcrowded, less than sea-worthy vessels, but in many cases the attempts ended in disaster. Nonetheless, some did succeed, and go on to live happy and productive lives. Those who were unable to exit the country faced serious circumstances of their own.

History would probably reveal that after the U.S. Civil War there was tremendous anger and subsequent sanctions toward those who seceded from the union. Likewise, those who supported the North Vietnam cause shunned South Vietnamese sympathizers. Quang told us that most of his friends who served in the South Vietnamese Army have had a tough life barely scratching out a living. The better jobs almost always went to those who supported the North's cause. Add to the equation that many of these individuals are limited in their ability to be productive because of combat wounds; not to mention there is no government pension or veterans' disability pension to compensate them for their military service connected disabilities.

The former North Vietnamese Army colonel we talked to in Hanoi expressed it best when he said, "These people, although allowed to vote, live very quiet lives. The true respect and appreciation must go to those who fought to keep a unified Vietnam. They are the ones that sacrificed to save their country and ensured the future of Vietnam."

A local government official in Vietnam with whom we spoke agreed, "These people should feel fortunate to enjoy life in this wonderful country."

Quang also agrees that his life and the lives of his former comrades are difficult ones. He knows that his life could and would be better had he not taken up arms against the government. He recognizes it will take another generation or two for his children's grandchildren to "catch up" economically with those who supported the north. Yet, when we asked Quang if he regretted his involvement with the United States troops and the American effort, he said with a straight face, "No."

We gave Quang twenty American dollars (a large sum in Vietnam currency) and told him to do something special with his family. It seemed like the least we could do for him.

CHAPTER 5

RICH OF DEFIANCE, OHIO
SILENT KILLER AND UNSUNG HERO

Rich's story really begins with what has turned out to be the true Ghoul Ghost and Phantom of Vietnam, the silent killer. It is no secret that methods to address jungle foliage by use of chemicals were heavily utilized in Vietnam. It would appear both the United States and Vietnam agree that approximately 70 million liters of the herbicide *Agent Orange* were sprayed across the central and southern regions of the southeast Asian country between 1964 and 1971. They further agree on two more specifics: (1) there are associated side-effects from exposure and (2) there are no simple answers to finding a resolution or method(s) to determine compensation. Vietnam contends that Vietnamese *Agent Orange* victims need help now! The United States stands on the premise that scientists need time. Vietnam, on the other hand, contends that victims cannot wait for definitive answers.

According to the Vietnam Government, most of the children affected by *Agent Orange* are those of parents who fought in the central battlefields south of the DMZ–in particular, the provinces of Quang Tri, Quang Nam (DaNang) and Tay Nguyen (Central Highlands). They further contend that their veterans stationed in their northern provinces north of the DMZ "do not report similar afflictions" with regard to offspring. Today, Vietnam government officials assert that the *Agent Orange* issue is not about money, but rather about ethics.

Through the help of Vietnam veterans and various organizations, the Vietnamese Government has established

Friendship Village. Friendship Village (opened in 1998) is a humanitarian facility designed to care for the children and elderly who are afflicted or have been born with congenital malformations and victims of the after effects of "toxic chemical spray warfare." The facility also serves as a center of research on treatment of certain diseases that many believe to be derived from the dioxin *Agent Orange*. While in Vietnam, we had the chance to talk to a couple of U.S. Vietnam vets, who had just visited the village. I will spare you their sickening, grotesque description of the tiny victims. However, the victims of *Agent Orange* do not end with the children and elderly of Friendship Village.

This is the story of Rich Cromwell, a sincere, humble, husband, father, grandfather, local elected public official, community volunteer, American, and Vietnam veteran who personifies the stature of placing the baby boomers in the domain for contention as also the "Greatest Generation."

Today, Rich lives with his wife of 38 years in a quiet rural area near the village of Ney, Ohio. Ney is located about 50 miles smack-dab between Ft. Wayne, Indiana and Toledo, Ohio. Today, he enjoys spending time with his daughter and two grandchildren. But Rich's life has not been all that easy. As a youngster, Rich experienced considerable hearing loss, a condition that was significantly aggregated by his U.S Army military service while serving in the Republic of Vietnam.

Rich logged countless hours of flight time on military fixed wing and helicopters, being shuttled between Camp Evans, near Phu Bia, and Da Nang in 1968. Exposure to gunfire blasts, the natural roar of military choppers' rotor blades negatively impacted his already deteriorating hearing condition. Today, Rich wears a hearing aid device and we all recognize that it is best when talking to him to always be face to face and speak loudly; no one has ever heard Rich complain, not even once, about his hearing loss.

The hearing loss is by far the less significant of his afflictions today. For you see, Rich was diagnosed with prostrate cancer, a result of being exposed to *Agent Orange* and had his prostrate removed. What amazed me about Rich was his attitude, always joking about his condition, making himself the butt of all his jokes.

In spite of all the unfavorable, unpleasant walls Rich had to face, he has never broke stride. Using the G.I. Bill, he received three degrees from post secondary institutions, including a B.S. Degree in Accounting from the prestigious Defiance College. Currently, Rich serves as the CEO of The Hubbard Company, a multi-million dollar printing company where he has worked for more than 30 years. Rich has run in marathons (26 miles 385 yards) in 48 of the 50 states and is scheduled to compete in Idaho and Maine. Recently, Rich handily won a three-way race for the Office of County Commissioner in Defiance County, Ohio, which means he will be leaving the elected post of township clerk that he has held for nineteen years.

Finally, he believes his great contributions to be the Christmas wreath sales that he instituted in the local Sertoma Club Organization, the proceeds of which go to purchasing hearing aid devices for those who cannot afford them. One of Rich's other greatest accomplishment is being one fine example to the youth and folks of our community.

CHAPTER 6

HOME FRONT SUPPORT EFFORT

We had them in great numbers in this country during WWII. I am talking about the people who went into the factories every day to produce much needed war materials. The people who walked to work, church and the market in order to conserve gas and reduce rubber wear, extending the life of automobile tires. The folks who put out gardens, reduced sugar consumption and went the extra mile for the good of the cause. The people who proudly displayed their flags, sending out that strong message of support to those involved in the tough job of battling the enemy. Yes indeed, we had many here at home, who stood tall for the war cause. It was the thing to do and nearly everyone did it!

May we suggest that we had these same types of highly patriotic people around during Vietnam? One such person is a woman called Mary Lee. Mary Lee falls somewhere between the WWII generation and the baby boomers. She was born in 1930 to parents who instilled strong values in her. Mary Lee's father taught her the importance of possessing a strong work ethic. He, himself, worked in a factory loading and unloading large quantities of steel shipments when it was done the old fashioned way– using a strong back! Her mother, on the other hand, taught Mary Lee the importance of prayer, which she duly passed on to her own children. Mary Lee had another influence in her life that in part established the patriotic streak. That influence was her Uncle Albert, a WWI Veteran who spent most of his post-war years living in a Veteran's Administration hospital getting around with the aid of a small electric cart.

While it is true that the Vietnam generation did not have to conserve rubber and sugar for the war effort, they did have to make decisions and did do many things that provided strong support to the troops. In Mary Lee's case, she prayed daily asking God to grant safety and protection for one of her children, serving in Vietnam. I suspect, since the beginning of time, nearly every mother having a child engaged in war prayed for the safe return of that child. Nonetheless, my guess is that Mary Lee prayed more intently than most, not only for her own, but also for all serving in the midst of the conflict. But Mary Lee's involvement did not stop there. She was soon to be faced with a dilemma requiring a decision every bit as difficult as walking instead of riding, conserving and going without as the WWII generation did. Unbeknown to her, that dilemma and her subsequent decision still continues to impact people in the name of America.

It was a hot August day in 1970, Mary Lee was running the vacuum sweeper, dusting and generally cleaning the house as she did nearly everyday of her adult life. A knock at the door caught her attention. Standing there were two neatly-dressed, clean-cut young men, each adorned in a white shirt and dark conservative necktie. Both of the young men were carrying what appeared to be leaflets or flyers in their hands. One of the young men introduced himself and his partner as members of the area Jehovah Witness Church and proceeded to tell Mary Lee about their beliefs. One of the things that they shared was that they would not join the military and under no circumstances would they fight in a war. They continued their presentation by asking Mary Lee if she would buy one of their publications called the *Watchtower*. Mary Lee said, "Why yes, I will buy the whole stack." The pair immediately broke into broad beaming smiles. She then asked them to excuse her for just a moment; she would only be a minute. The anxious pair eagerly awaited her return and must have been surprised when she returned not only with her purse, but also holding a small American flag. She then said, "I will buy all of your *Watchtowers* if you will salute this flag, for you see, I have a son serving in the Marines in Vietnam." Their smiles turned to looks of seriousness, "We can't salute the flag!"

"Well then," Mary Lee said boldly, "I cannot purchase any of your *Watchtowers*!"

This is a true story because Mary Lee is my mom and I, W. Tom Wiseman, was that young Marine. Mom later went on to become active in the American Legion Auxiliary, VWF Auxiliary and now the AMVETS Auxiliary. Over the years she has had heart bypass surgery, and her appendix and gallbladder removed. She has had a complete hysterectomy, major colon and kidney surgery. Yet, at age 74 and quite frail, on many Saturdays, gets up, drives to AMVETS Post 1991 (arriving at 6:00 A.M.) so she can lead the group for Saturday morning breakfast sales to raise money for those less fortunate veterans and their families. In her most recent report as third vice, at the July 16th meeting of the AMVETS Auxiliary Post 1991, she reported her fund raising projects to benefit veterans, which included: Paws with a Cause, Veteran's Christmas Baskets, and Eyeglass Collections, (including parts and cases), helping at the Senior Center and participating in the Hospice Walk in May. Additionally, she reported that she had received 1,032 cancelled stamps from the auxiliary to date. It is with pleasure that we proudly nominate Mary Lee for membership to the ranks of "Our Hero Generation!"

Mom's action, regarding the flag, lives on impacting people to this very day because I teach American National Government at Bowling Green State University, The Defiance College, as well as history at Northwest State Community College, Archbold, Ohio. In these classes the discussion ultimately revolves to the subjects of Vietnam and patriotism. I have been teaching college since

1997 and cannot remember even one course in which I did not share the *Watchtower*, American flag story. My guess is that some of the students will remember the courage that Mom displayed in the name of our flag, and might even pass the story on to others at some point in their lives–perhaps even to their own children!

CHAPTER 7

ANGELS REALLY DO EXIST…

Exploratory research in 1993 has offered evidence to support the notion that most women's lives are greatly affected by the violence they experience. Terri's experience happened when support for domestic violence was not strong in her small community. It was kept behind closed doors where the violence took place. Nobody wanted to get involved. Just keep quiet, they told her. Terri was married to a Vietnam veteran whom she loved very deeply. She was 21 and getting ready to graduate from college. He was 27, and had just returned home from the war. He would not talk much about his experiences in Vietnam, but did take her to the movie "Deer Hunter," which he said was an example of what happened in the Vietnam War. After she saw the movie she was devastated by what many of our soldiers might have gone through fighting in this war. Although he never talked much about his personal experiences, she assumed they had affected his thoughts and actions. Prior to his war experiences he was altogether different. Many would say he was a kinder gentler person. Terri graduated from college and got her first teaching job. Now life was going to be wonderful… she thought.

The domestic violence started with a shove up against the refrigerator. After the first incident, every one that followed became more brutal. After the abuse, he was always sorry and loving. There were so many incidents in which he would totally tear down her self-esteem. He knew he could do it to her and destory her spirit. She stayed and thought she would try harder.

She had to give in, to stay silent, and continue to stay silent so her child wouldn't see or hear any more violent outbursts. Sometimes everything would be going fine and all of a sudden something she said or did was wrong. He would come home from work and tear apart the bed because she didn't make it with his expected military corners. He would re-vacuum the carpet because he would see a speck of dust. She tried to clean the house perfectly, but it was never right. She would go to work wearing dark glasses. On one occasion, her principal sent her home and told her not to come back until her bruises were healed. It was her first year of teaching and at the end of that year she was rifted. She always felt it was because of her constant emotional problems from home and her diminishing self-esteem.

Many times she complained to the police, but they supported her husband and told her they did not want to be involved in family matters. The abuse made her determined to get through her problems, like, nothing is going to get in her way, you know, of living her dream and being a successful teacher. She didn't want to see her children or any children get hurt. Terri's abuse ended after she spent a week in the hospital with a ruptured spleen, many facial cuts, bruises, and a broken heart. Her physician told her, "Next time he is going to kill you; get out now!"

She went home from the hospital only to pack while he was at work. She contacted a lawyer, moved to an apartment and filed a restraining order to keep him away. This was one of the most difficult decisions she had ever made. She felt like a failure at life for not being able to keep her husband happy.

Terri has gone on with her life. She has been happily married for twenty years and has an adult son, two great teenagers and two wonderful grandchildren. She has obtained her Master of Arts Degree and recently a Ph.D. in Education; she continues to teach. With bittersweet memories of her past, she often wonders if he had not gone through the violence in Vietnam maybe his aggressions would not have surfaced.

Few would argue against the fact that Terri was one of the prettiest eighth graders in the entire Jr. High School, not only physically pleasing, but always upbeat, fun-loving and just plain pleasant to be around. Having lost contact with Terri after high school graduation, it was not until working on my dissertation that we reconnected. It was then that the truth of her abuse, misery and pain at the hands of a war-torn husband came to light. It was indeed a sad thing to learn about her horrible experience. For many, the story would end there! Yet, for Terri, there existed an internal desire not to become another casuality, but rather felt an inherent need to "break the cycle."

Terri could have easily thrown up her hands giving up on the human race as well as herself. Rather, she became more intent than ever to help those in need. She concentrated her efforts and directed her love to her students–youngsters having special needs. As an elementary teacher, Terri worked hard to organize a number of special individualized reading programs and interventions to aid struggling students. Rumor has it that Terri regularly provided economically disadvantaged students with food, clothing and everyday necessities to ensure that they would have at least a "fighting chance." By some accounts, Terri has positively influenced many hundreds and even thousands of young lives. In many cases, these youngsters–particularly at risk youngsters–have gone on to become strong family promoters and productive community leaders.

Yes, Terri became a highly respected icon as an educator who went beyond the call of duty. She ensures that the neglected, struggling child knows his or her own worth. But Terri did not quit there! Today, a Doctor of Philosophy, she is highly respected in the field of education and considered a leader in the discipline of Educational Technology. Not only has Terri devoted a large part of her free time, talents and the majority of her life to struggling children, but also she has even succeeded beyond that great accomplishment. She has triumphed to what many agree is the supreme accomplishment one might achieve in this world. She has truly forgiven the one whose violent acts nearly destroyed her, nearly killed her. Yes indeed, Terri is truly by all accounts a worthy candidate for membership to "Our Hero Generation."

CHAPTER 8

BEARING FRUIT
OUR DEATH PRODUCES FRUIT

"Amen, amen, I say to you, unless the grain of wheat falls into the ground and dies, it remains alone. But if it dies, it brings forth much fruit." (St. John Ch.12 vs. 24 & 25). Three significant dates stand out in the mind of Tommy and Pauline Love. They are May 26th, 1947, August 28th, 1967 and the year 1991. To most of us parents, the source of our greatest pride and joy is our children. Tommy and Pauline were no exception. The Loves fondly remember that cold winter day when little Gary was born. He weighed a whole 7 lbs. Most of Tommy and Pauline's memories about Gary are from his childhood and his wonderful ability to get along with others.

The news on August 28, 1967, that sad, earth-shattering day for the Loves, came via a telegram. This devastating news that their beloved son Gary was killed in action as a result of a hostile land mine explosion in a providence in Vietnam.

Yes, three significant dates stand out in the Love's minds. They are the day Gary was born into their life, the day Gary was killed in action, and the day the American Veterans, (AMVETS) Post 1991 located in Defiance, Ohio was chartered into existence. And this is where Paul Harvey would step-up to the microphone and say, "Here is the rest of the story..."

AMVETS Post 1991 proudly bestows the name of Gary. Oh, not just Gary but it does include Gary's name. The post is named after three young heroes: Kenneth Grahm, Dean Hancock and Gary Love. Three brave men who gave their all and made the supreme sacrifice, fighting for those oppressed people in another part of the world, defending the values of freedom.

But the true source of Tommy and Pauline's joy is the many wonderful things done by so few, for so many in need. AMVETS Post 1991, Defiance, Ohio, since its existence, has raised hundreds of thousands of dollars, and has helped countless numbers of people in need. Hungry people, cold people, lonely people; like the scores of many aged veterans found in the Ohio Veteran's Home in Sandusky, Ohio. They support not only the needs of veterans but also the needs of their widows and dependent children. They hold regularly Saturday morning fundraisers to ensure that poor and often neglected little children receive at least a gift on Christmas morning.

Yes, Pauline and Tommy look long past and far beyond that dreadful August day in 1967 half-way around the world. Everyday Gary's parents thank God for their son's great sacrifice; and the wonderful humanitarian deeds that have resulted in Gary's name.

The Loves took a sad, painful and tragic event, and turned it into what most every religion tries to instill, the act of forgiveness… and so, as Paul Harvey would say, "Now you know the rest of the story."

CHAPTER 9

DAN'S STORY
PRISON DE HOA LO

The Prison De Hoa Lo as the infamous "Hanoi Hilton." The prison built in 1896 is located in the City of Hanoi and has an interesting history. Actually, much of the original structure has been razed and or renovated to accommodate capital growth. A major portion is now dedicated as a business center.

The history of the prison is found in a brochure titled "Vestige Historique." The following is a description of the prisons history as written and approved by the Government of Vietnam:

> "In the end of the XIX century, in order to cope with more and more increasing fighting movement of Vietnamese people, French colony reinforced its suppression apparatus by policies, courts and prisons. The Hoa Lo Prison was built up in 1896, which was the biggest one of the Northern Indo-China.
>
> From a reputed traditional profession-village, this Hoa Lo land became a place to imprison and ground down thousands of patriots and revolutionary fighters physically and spiritually. Many of them sacrificed their lives to independence and freedom of the nation.
>
> Kept in prison cells with chain, bare-handed patriots and revolutionist yet fought against draconian custody regime, harsh living and savage suppression by the French colony; kept high sense of purpose and uprightness stand; turned the prison into a revolutionary

> organization school; sought every way to escape from the jail return to the people, revolutionary organizations and made worthy contribution to the revolution.
>
> The North was liberated in October 1954 and Hoa Lo prison was used by the Vietnam state to imprison legal violators. From August 5, 1964 to March 31, 1973, the Hoa Lo prison kept part of American pilots where planes had been shot down while bombing, bombarding and causing crimes to North Vietnam people."

Since 1973, in order to address the developing needs of the capital city, Vietnam Authority decided to change the Hoa Lo scope of use: a part of the Hoa Lo prison (facing Hoa Lo street) is scheduled to be restored, upgraded and now is recognized as a Historic Relic; the other part is to be built up to become a business center. Today, one can view the various instruments of torture as well as the "head-cutting machine" (guillotine). According to the literature, the machine was used on many patriots and revolutionists. One can also view propaganda pictures of American prisoners of war (POW's) along with the only remaining cell that was furnished and used by Americans. The cell contained a rack (bed) covered with what appeared to be a thin woven mat.

The pictures on the wall, show our POW's preparing a meal, receiving letters and Christmas gifts from home as well as reverently praying in a church. We overheard one French woman explain as she left the compound: "I didn't realize they treated the American POW's so well." While we do believe the pictures are probably authentic; likewise, we believe such incidents were very rare indeed. Nonetheless, the place was still a cold, damp miserable setting. Rebo and I did do something to honor the brave Americans who stood tall for their country and endured the years of psychological and physical torment. We rolled up a small

American Flag and dropped it into a deep crevice in the concrete cell wall, where it will likely never be discovered. It left us with a good feeling knowing the Stars and Stripes of Old Glory will remain there in honor of those who gave unselfishly of their-selves.

The March day that we visited the prison, the temperature and humidity was like one of those hot, muggy Ohio summer days when you perspire just sitting, standing or doing nothing at all. Actually, the dampness of the prison was a relief from the scorching heat. As we completed our tour, we bumped into a Caucasian, English speaking gentlemen dressed in a combination of Vietnamese and western attire. He asks, "Where are you from?" I responded, "The United States." "I know," he said, "I heard you talking! I mean from where in the U.S.?" We told him Ohio. We couldn't help but notice that he stood in a somewhat strange manner, with one leg straight up and down and the other at what appeared to be forty-degree angle. Rebo asked him what his name was and where he was from. He told us his name was Dan and he was from Oregon. We talked and asked him what he was doing in Vietnam? His answer: *"Reclaiming my soul."*

As the sweat beaded up on his forehead and the obvious discomfort of the sweaty stump sliding around in the opening of his prosthetic device, Dan told us this story. In 1971, while on the last patrol and on the last day he was to be in Vietnam. (He said he could even see the landing-zone where the chopper was to come in and pick up his unit, it would take him back to the rear where he would then pack his gear and return to the U.S.) as his unit walked over a small knoll, they were ambushed and he was severely wounded. Dan lost his left leg well above the knee.

So, again we asked Dan, "What are you doing here?"

"Truly fellows, I have returned to *reclaim my soul*!" He then explained, that he and four other gentlemen (all Vietnam veterans) were refurbishing a run down orphanage. I saw a tear in the corner of Rebo's eye.

To think, after all these years of suffering and to truly help the enemy that destroyed their lives, they were finding peace in helping the children. We shook hands and wished each other well as we walked through the prison gates. The arrector pili muscles formed goose bumps on what seemed like every inch of my body and my thoughts were simply that forgiveness is indeed, to know peace. Privately, I asked the Lord to help me to become more like Dan, a true hero.

CHAPTER 10

TRULY, A REAL HERO'S WELCOME

Some gifts just seem to have more meaning than others. You know that little homemade construction paper cutout of a Christmas tree your second grader made for you. The one that hung on the refrigerator door so long that the sides curled up making it appear more like an oversized paper-wad. The one that you treasured, you remember, the one with sort of an odd shape that looked more like a disjointed jellyfish and had those crayon scribbles that followed absolutely no pattern and resembled the formation of spilled Kool-Aid on the countertop. The one that melted your heart and that you would not have parted with for all the rice in China. Well, my friend Bill in chapter one received his homemade Christmas tree on Father's Day 2003.

The only difference is that this homemade gift came from his twenty-one-year-old daughter, Janna. A senior at Bowling Green State University, who participated in the "Semester at Sea Program" with one of the calls of port being Vietnam. Janna's trip, along with Bill and his wife's desire to visit Janna, ultimately resulted in getting our Vietnam visit off the ground.

No matter how yellow the white paper becomes and how much the corners roll up into a big ball, it is our guess that this one will hang on the refrigerator door for a long time.

A DIFFERENT SIDE OF MY DAD

If someone were to say the word 'dad' to me I would automatically think of a man in a suit and tie heading off the work in the morning. I would think of someone coming home just in time for dinner and wanting to know all the details of my day, someone to watch TV with in the evenings and go to sporting events with on the weekends, and someone to laugh with about everything and share old stories with. I would think about someone who has shown me the world in so many ways, supported everything I have ever done, and loved me unconditionally for it.

Thoughts that would have never come to my head would have been a man dressed in army fatigues throwing grenades. I would never have thought about him sitting in rice patties worried about who may sneak up on him during the night. I can't imagine him shooting a gun or doing any other harmful thing. But these are all things that I learned that my father once did.

Although I always knew that my dad was a Vietnam veteran, I never really knew what that meant until I was able to see it with my own eyes. He would tell me a story here and there, but it was something that we did not usually speak about. Looking back now, I feel that this is something that he may have been hiding from us in order to protect us. I don't think that my dad wanted us to know everything that he had to go through and probably never wants us to have to experience it. While traveling through the villages in Vietnam with my dad, he finally let me in to this aspect of his life.

As we traveled through the countryside in our old mini bus I didn't know what to expect. I wasn't sure what I was about to see or how everyone would react. We drove for miles and miles and I heard many stories about the different mountains we were passing. I heard about towers that were once placed at the top of them for radio connection and about how the soldiers climbed over them to ambush the Viet Cong. Finally, we were able to find the dirt road that led back to the village where my dad had been stationed. We drove on the rocky road a long way back until we finally stopped, got out of the mini-bus, and my dad looked around. You could see in his eyes the transportation back to 1970. He quickly looked around to see what had changed and if he could remember anything. We saw a lady working outside her house and asked if we could enter her yard. As we got closer we noticed a well outside and my dad told us that was one like they built while he was there. There was also a shower next to it and my dad got out an old picture of him showering, it was exactly like the one we were standing next to.

Soon we had people gathered all around us wanting to help us. There was one man who was tall, very skinny, and didn't speak a word of English. Because our driver could speak both languages we were able to communicate with him. He told us that he was 16 during the war and he remembered the bombs and gunshots. He also kept saying that there was a man with black skin and he pointed to an area very near us where this man had been shot. I could tell by the look in my dad's eyes that the story was true. He then took out a picture of him and this man and showed it to the Vietnamese man, and at that moment they connected. Although it was very sad to think about these things happening, it was awesome to see that my dad was able to come back and find ways in order to create closure for himself.

While my dad took off on a motorcycle in order to go and search for one last site, I walked around the village a while. I couldn't believe it, but I felt a bit like a celebrity. All the children came out to greet me and followed me around. I was proud to think that my father played a part in bettering the lives of these children. Even though they didn't have a lot of material things they all seemed happy and carefree. Although I still don't completely understand the war, I do know what my dad was doing there was right. I am proud to say that my father fought for our country and helped his fellow humans who were in need. He was pulled out after only four and a half months and he was really upset and wanted to stay. When he first told me this, I couldn't understand why someone would want to stay in a war zone, but now after seeing everything that he was doing it makes complete sense to me.

Now when someone mentions the word 'dad' to me, instead of just thinking about a businessman who has always put a roof over my head and clothes on my body, I will think of a war hero as well. A hero who doesn't have a purple heart or other medals, but someone who risked his life to better the lives of others. That is what I consider a hero to be.

Love,
Your daughter

CHAPTER 11

"OUR HERO GENERATION"

The "baby boomers" are said to be those who were born between the period of 1946 and 1964. Tom Brokaw's book *The Greatest Generation* refers to the WWII generation as the "Greatest Generation" because they were able to come together and unite in the form of tremendous personal commitment to the war effort. Brokaw believes this generation was bound by duty, honor, courage, service and love of country. In part, what makes them heroes and heroines is that they faced crisis such as the depression and the war and did it with humility. This generation faced these great odds and did not protest.

We would submit that this "Greatest Generation" might very well have united in cause, because it was the "thing to do." Consider this, the Japanese on the morning of December 7, 1941 did intentionally and maliciously bomb the U.S. military fleet and base at Pearl Harbor, Hawaii. This was a direct and intentional attack against the citizens and military personnel of the United States of America, thus offering a pretty damn good reason for the American people to come together. Yet, did the baby boomers do anything less with Vietnam, generation X with the Gulf War or the War on Terrorism? The fact is patriotism; duty; honor and courage were never greater! It's very much like being a supporter of a winning baseball team. Let's face it, when the team is winning the crowds swell. But, when the team is in a slump… This point can be best illustrated in the case of the former professional baseball team, the Washington Senators. In the last year of their existence as a major league team they could barely buy a win and tallied an average attendance of 500 per home game. It has been suggested that some of the team, at that time, simply gave up while others played harder than ever. Likewise, was the dilemma of the American youth of the 1960's and 70's dealing with Vietnam. Just like the Washington Senators, caught up in an unpopular situation. Yet, for two million of these hero baby boomers, even though support was sparse, they did not waiver. They displayed every bit of courage duty, honor, service and love of country that any of the "greatest generation" ever did, and not without insight. Let us consider their story.

While it is true that the annointed "Greatest Generation" faced difficult circumstances as the Depression and WWII and were indeed a fine generation of Americans. Can we consider the plight of the baby boomer generation? We must ask did our generation face anything less. The baby boomers were spun from a world war and many were saddled with the Korean Conflict while having their fathers taken away at an extremely needy and vulnerable time in their life. They lived through the Cuban Missile Crisis, the Cold War, at a time when the world was on the brink of nuclear destruction and annihilation. Instead of having fire drills and tornado drills in school, these young children were repeatedly required to go through crawling under their desks, forcing their heads into their laps, and shielding the top of their head and face with their hands in preparation for a possible nuclear attack. If all of this is not enough, consider the fact that these boomers as young children were the first generation to truly find themselves "Home Alone" because their mothers, in part, due to economic necessity, chose to remain out of the home and in the factories and if all of this challenge were not enough these boomers as young children were exposed to being reared in more broken single family homes from the birth of this nation up to that time, as the national divorce rate in the years following World War II. The divorce rate has steadily increased from around one per thousand to around 4.5 per thousand. As previously suggested, the choice for baby boomers regarding Vietnam was not so clear-cut! The WWII generation decision was, in fact, a no-brainer. We were attacked and we defended. The Vietnam baby boomers, on the other hand, had to make a choice between duty and conscience. For example:

- 9,087,000 military personnel served on active duty during the Vietnam era (Aug 5, 1964-May 7, 1975).
- 8,744,000 GIs were on active duty during the war (Aug 5, 1964-March 28, 1973).
- 3,403,100 (including 514,300 offshore) personnel served in the Southeast Asia Theater (Vietnam, Laos, Cambodia, flight crews based in Thailand, and sailors in adjacent South China Sea waters).
- 2,594,000 personnel served within the borders of South Vietnam (Jan. 1, 1965-March 28, 1973). Another 50,000 served in Vietnam between 1960 and 1964.
- Of the 2.6 million, between 1 and 1.6 million (40-60%) either fought in combat, provided close support or was at least fairly regularly exposed to enemy attack.
- 7,484 women (6,250 or 83.5% were nurses) served in Vietnam.
- Peak troop strength in Vietnam: 543,482 (April 30, 1969). Many made the choice of duty to enter and serve in the Armed Forces of the United States between 1964 and 1974.

What made Vietnam so different was the speed in which combatants were exposed, creating a certain element of cultural shock. For example, for the most part, during WWII, ships from the U.S. to their assigned theater or destination transported

American service personnel. This meant travel time of days, weeks and even longer. An incredibly valuable time to reflect, prepare and adjust. Vietnam combat soldiers, on the other hand, were exposed to the "JET AGE"! In the matter of a few short hours, these combat personnel were transported from the U.S. to the jungles of Vietnam. We talked to one individual who was caught in an ambush and in just a few short hours was sitting in a fast food restaurant in California. In my own case, I can recall the flash of the howitzers, tracer bullets and enemy rockets in the darkness of night as we flew out of DaNang. Then in couple of hours, you were watching and listening to Ray Stevens, on T.V. in Okinawa, singing, "Everything is Beautiful." What an adjustment!

The point is simply this, every generation may well be the "Greatest Generation" given the time and circumstance, and the Vietnam era Americans are no exception. While there was expressed opposition during the Vietnam conflict that greatly exceeded the WWII era nonetheless, during Vietnam not even the opposing sides totally disagreed. Those who chose military service and those who chose to be conscientious objectors very much agreed on one major point. There were serious political screw-ups. The point was simply that the failure of Vietnam is directly attributed to the poor leadership by then America's top leaders. Perhaps Neil Sheean, author of *A Bright Shining Lie* said it best, "In WWII you had leadership, people who knew what they were doing."

So just exactly what did the individuals who served in Vietnam and those who opposed the war accomplish? The answers are several. Clearly, we minimized, if not completely eradicated the domino theory concern. Secondly, they taught us a valuable lesson, a lesson that we have applied to every single conflict that has occurred since. What we learned is that we must tell the American people why we are engaging in a conflict, have a clear mission and most important an exit strategy. Unlike WWII, Vietnam has not received a positive historical place in history. Actually, many would like to forget that Vietnam ever happened. Today there are still 1,600 Americans missing in action and we have an obligation and must continue to tell our story. It is like the Holocaust, the Jewish people built a museum, and they will not let the world forget! Should Vietnam veterans do anything less?

So, what is the value of returning to your place of war? The answers are: it offers a number of distinct opportunities as well as a second chance. Remember the demon that has been haunting you all of these years? Returning offers the opportunity to discover that Vietnam is no longer a war, but rather, it is a country. Remember when you returned to the States and there were no ticker tape parades or appreciative people waiting your return? A second trip provides an excellent opportunity for the homecoming you never had. In my case, I was welcomed at the Toledo airport by excited family members including my brother Tim who was age five when I was stationed in Vietnam and his son, Joel Wiseman, who was born in 1987.

Returning to Vietnam not only allows you to purge the demons, but it also provides a wonderful opportunity to "Reclaim the Soul." Yet, even if you choose not to return to Vietnam, there is something that *every* one of us can and must do and that is to make certain our generation finds its due place in history, as yet another one of the "greatest hero generations" of all.

CHAPTER 12

WHY NOT CONSIDER RECLAIMING YOUR SOUL?

So, just exactly what does it mean to reclaim the soul? How might one go about doing such a thing and moreover, why would anyone want to do it? The answers are many but the reason is one. There are an estimated three hundred million people in these United States. While it is true, one can find random despicable accounts of appalling behavior in most every newspaper and news broadcast, it does not take a rocket scientist to recognize that there is, by far more good in this world. Thus, you already have the advantage of yearning for good over evil. Additionally, as human beings we long for and seek peace of mind. *Reclaiming the Soul* is really about giving of ones self. It is about forgiving others and it is about helping others and in doing so we can achieve the ultimate personal fulfillment that most people desire, the joy of inner peace.

Volunteerism is good for the soul. The strongest human heart is found within a volunteer. Reclaiming the Soul is just that. For true peace, that passes all human understanding is to be had not in retreat from any battle but to travel any journey for the sake of saving our own lives. Little by little to cease to live, in any sense that matters is only discovery for the sake of the world, even when the world irks, sickens and shocks us, that we start to come alive and reclaim our soul. It is like carrying a torch through life, we should burn as bright as we can during our brief moment in time.

There is evidence from research proving that there are healing benefits of volunteering. The "Helper's High" is a term coined by Allan Luks author of, *The Healing Power of Doing Good.* In the mid 1980's Allan Luks, executive director of Big Brothers Big Sisters of New York City, conducted a survey of 3,300 volunteers. His research stated that many volunteers experience feelings of euphoria while volunteering. He calls this the helper's high. The volunteers also describe a good physical feeling. They compare it to the runner's high - when a person runs and exerts, but instead of feeling more stressed, they feel more relaxed. Their act of helping caused both a physiological and an emotional effect on the volunteers.

The Helper's high is hypothesized to function similarly to the runner's high by stimulating the release of endorphins, that are natural hormones that help improve mood and also help to improve the body's immune system. Research has shown that volunteering on a regular basis improves self-esteem, increases your sense of well-being, and lowers stress. So helping others through volunteering can be beneficial to our health. It can also produce a helper's calm, feelings of calm and well being that continue for hours after volunteering. We believe with the new millennium, a person will no longer be judged by how much he/she owns or possesses, but rather by their contribution to the community. We encourage you to try volunteering, to give of yourself, to see the joy in someone's eyes, a smile on a child or an elder's face, the feeling of contentment in the heart. Then you, too, will begin to understand why our "greatest hero generation" chose to volunteer, like Dan, to reclaim their soul. The harder we work for others the more we live.

"Never doubt that a small group of thoughtful citizens can change the world. Indeed, it is the only thing that ever has...."
— Margaret Mead

Forgiveness is really a combination of compassion, kindness, understanding and sympathy toward others. It means looking for the best in others, even those who have hurt us the most. Life is not always fair! Yet, when we fail to forgive, we allow that person or persons to live rent-free in our mind. When we forgive and help others we change lives, including our own!

Reclaiming the Soul is really about making a commitment to you. It is a feeling! It is about conscience and good over evil. It is seeing the best in others. It is about letting go! It is about forgiving yourself. As previously mentioned, it is about changing lives! The people in our book are not one bit different than you or us, except for one thing. The people in our book all displayed the most powerful force in life! That force is faith and love. They have turned negatives into positives. You too can be anything you want to be and do anything you want to do in life. Just as the people in our book, you too can give your self a second chance. After all, how many times have you heard someone say, "Boy, if I could just have the chance to do it over?" Well now you can, you can give yourself that second chance! Set your goals high. No matter what your Vietnam is in this life. Be a positive example to others, especially our greatest natural resource, our youth! Make a positive influence on the lives of others by forgiving and helping them. For in doing so you will know no greater joy or peace of mind, for you will have then RECLAIMED YOUR SOUL!